BEGINNING
BARITONE
UKULELE BOOTCAMP

UKELIKETHEPROS
© 2019 TERRY CARTER

ISBN-13: **978-0-9826151-8-8**
UKELIKETHEPROS.COM
© 2019 TERRY CARTER

TABLE OF CONTENTS

BEGINNING
BARITONE
UKULELE BOOTCAMP

The Beginning Baritone Bootcamp book by Terry Carter is perfect for the beginning ukulele or guitar player who is ready to master the songs and essential fundamentals necessary to become the best baritone ukulele player that you can be.

Do you know how the baritone ukulele is different from the soprano, concert, and tenor ukuleles? Have you struggled finding instructional material for the baritone ukulele? If you have asked yourself these questions, then the Beginning Baritone Ukulele Bootcamp book by Terry Carter is going to be perfect for you.

Terry Carter and Uke Like The Pros have some great online ukulele courses out there. The Beginning Baritone Ukulele Bootcamp book will provide you with a step-by-step baritone ukulele tutorial instruction that will give you the necessary tools to learn to play your favorite songs. Give you a full understanding of the tuning and the chords used on the baritone ukulele so that you can not only follow youtube videos but also properly play with other ukulele players using soprano, concert, or tenor ukuleles.

Baritone ukuleles are tuned D - G - B - E (low to high), while soprano, concert, and tenor ukuleles are tuned G - C - E - A (low to high).

Since the baritone ukulele is different not only in size, sound, and strings as the soprano, concert, and tenor ukuleles you'll get a solid foundation to master this awesome instruments.

With over 30 years as an educator, master instructor Terry Carter will bring his proven teaching method that has helped thousands of people learn the ukulele, many just like you.Discover the chords necessary to play the songs you always wanted to play.Develop amazing right hand technique.

The strumming hand is the most important hand when playing the ukulele. I will show you techniques that will help you develop speed, strength, and dexterity.Develop a strong sense of rhythm and time with the downloadable backing tracks. You'll get a logical and methodical system for learning the baritone ukulele. Grow confidence in your playing and you are learning the right things.

The Beginning Baritone Ukulele book is broken up into 4 categories.

PART ONE: The Essentials - Everything you need to know to properly play the baritone, understand music (even if your a beginner), and build your confidence as a musician.

PART TWO: Songs - Songs are one of the most important things to start because they teach you how to play and memorize chords, how to strum, how to smoothing transition from chord to chord, and have fun as you are learning parts from your favorite songs.

PART THREE: Next Level Songs - You have to break out of your comfort zone and start challenging yourself. This section is perfect at push your playing to new levels as you and others hear a difference in the way you sound on the baritone ukulele.

PART FOUR: Scales - Scales are essential to know because they build your technique and speed as you get comfortable going up and down the strings and the baritone neck. Once you get your scales down you can start creating your own melodies that will for sure turn the heads of those listening.

Weather your a beginner baritone ukulele or guitar player the Beginning Baritone Ukulele Bootcamp book will help you become the best baritone ukulele player that you can be.

Are you ready?

It's now your turn to dive into the *Beginning Baritone Ukulele Bootcamp Book.*

LESSON 01 | **YOUR FIRST CHORD**

This lesson uses the "G", chord with all downstrokes and whole notes.
Make sure to let the whole notes ring out for 4 beats.

LESSON 02 | **THE E MINOR CHORD**

This lesson uses the "E" minor chord with all downstrokes and half notes.
Half notes ring out for 2 beats and you will strum on beats 1 and 3.

LESSON 03 | **THE C CHORD**

This lesson uses the "C" chord with all downstrokes and quarter notes.
Quarter notes ring out for 1 beat and you will strum on beats 1, 2, 3, and 4.

LESSON 04 | **THE D CHORD**

This lesson introudces the "D" chord and uses quarter notes and half notes.
You will strum on beats 1, 2, and 3, and then let the chord ring out over beat 4. Use all downstrokes.

LESSON 05 | **COMBINING RHYTHMS**

This lesson uses the "G" chord with all downstrokes. This will review your quarter, half, and whole notes. You will play each rhythm for 2 measures. Make sure not to rush the quarter notes.

1 + 2 + 3 + 4 +   *Sim...*

LESSON 06 | **2 CHORDS: G AND E MINOR**

This lesson uses the "G" and "E minor" chords with all downstrokes and whole notes.
The easiest way to switch from chord to chord is memorize these chords.

1 + 2 + 3 + 4 + *Sim...*

LESSON 07 | G AND C CHORDS

This lesson uses the "G" and the "C" chords with all downstrokes and half notes.
Notice that you will switch chords every measure. Try to switch chords without looking at your fretboard.

LESSON 08 | E MINOR AND C CHORDS

This lesson uses the "E minor" and "C" chords with all downstrokes and quarter notes.
Notice you only have to add the 1st finger to go from the "E minor" to the "C" chord.

LESSON 09 | G AND D CHORDS

This lesson uses the "G" and "D" chords with all downstrokes and whole notes.
The whole notes make it easier to get to the "D" chord, which is one of the harder open-position chords.

LESSON 10 | 4 CHORDS WITH D7

This lesson uses the "G", "E minor", "C", and "D7" chords using half notes. Each chord will be played 2 times per measure on beats 1 and 3. Notice when you go from the "C" chord to the "D7" chord you do not have to lift your 1st finger off the string.

LESSON 11 | **LET IT BE PROGRESSION**

This lesson uses the "G", "D", "E minor", and "C" chords with all downstrokes and whole notes.
Notice to get from the "E minor" to the "C" chord you only have to add your 1st finger on the 2nd string.

LESSON 12 | **4 CHORDS WITH B MINOR**

This lesson uses the "G", "Bmin", "Emin", and "C" chords. Although you switch chords every measure the half note on
beat 3 gives you a little time to get ready for the new chord. Use all downstrokes and you will
strum on beats 1, 2, and 3 but let the half note on beat 3 ring out for beat 4.

LESSON 13 | 4 CHORDS WITH A MINOR

This lesson uses the "G", "C", "D7", and introduces the "A minor" chord.
Notice how the "C", "A minor", and "D7" chords all have the 1st finger on the 2nd string, 1st fret.

LESSON 14 | THE UP STROKE

This lesson uses the "A minor", "C", "G", and "D" chords and introduces the 1/8th note strum pattern.
The 1/8th notes happen on beat 2 and you will strum with a downstroke on beat 2 and and an upstroke on the + of 2.
Typically, but not always, 1/8th notes are strummed with a down-up pattern.

LESSON 15 | **3 CHORDS - D DU D D**

In this lesson you will strum on every beat with 1/8th notes on beat 2 using a down-up pattern. Since you don't have a lot of time to switch chords, get- ting the chords memorized and looking ahead as you play will help make the changes faster and easier.

LESSON 16 | **INTRODUCING THE B7 CHORD**

This lesson introduces 2 new chords the "B7" and the "E7." The first measure also has 2 chords in it, the "G" and the "B7," The strum pattern uses quarter notes on beats 1, 2, and 4 and 1/8th notes on beat 3. Practice the 1st measure until you can switch smoothly between the "G" and "B7" chords.

This lesson introduces 2 new chords, the "E" and "A" chords. This is an important strum pattern to get down, as it can be used in many songs. It used 1/4th notes on beats 1 and 3, and 1/8 notes on beats 2 and 4.

LESSON 18 | **THE BLUES**

This lesson is a 12-bar blues, and uses all 7th chord: the "·7", "A7", and "B7" chords. The Blues is one of the most important forms you need to understand as it connects all musical styles. This also uses what I call the "Granddaddy" strum pattern, which uses a tie (hold) between beats 2 and the + of 2.

LESSON 19 | D MAJOR SCALE OPEN

The Major scale is one of the most widely used scales for all styles of music, especially for rock, blues, country, and pop.
This scale is in the open position, which means that you will use open strings as the lowest notes.
It is very important to memorize these scales using the proper fingerings.

D Major Scale
(Open Position)

LESSON 20 | D MAJOR SCALE UP THE NECK

This is an alternate fingering for the D Major scale that uses 3 notes per string.
It is still in the open position since the lowest note you play is an open string.

D Major Scale
(Open Position)

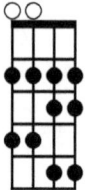

LESSON 21 | E MAJOR SCALE CLOSED

This E Major scale is in the closed position because it does not use any open strings. The nice thing about closed position scales is that you can slide this shape up and down the neck to play any Major scale in any key.

E Major Scale
(Closed Position)

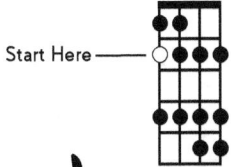

Start Here

Fingering 2 4 1 2   4 1 3 4   1 3 4 3   1 4 3 1   4 2 1 4   2 1 2

```
T|------------------2-4-5-4---2-------5-4-2-------------------------------|
A|------------2-4-5-------------------------4-2-1-----------------|
B|--2-4---1-2-4-------------------------------------4-2-1-2-------|
```

LESSON 22 | D MINOR PENTATONIC SCALE

The Minor Pentatonic is one of the most widely used scales for all styles of music, especially for blues, rock, funk, and jazz. This scale is in the open position because the lowest note you play is an open string. It is very important to memorize this scale using the proper fingerings.

D Minor Pentatonic Scale
(Open Position)

Fingering   3   2   1   3   1   3   1   3   1   2   3

```
T|----------------------1-3---1-------3-1-----------------|
A|----------------1-3---------------3-1---2---0-----------|
B|--0---3---0---2-------------------------------3---0-----|
```

LESSON 23 | **F MINOR PENTATONIC SCALE**

This F Minor Pentatonic scale is in the closed position because it does not use any open strings.
The nice thing about closed position scales is that you can slide this shape up and down
the neck to play any Minor Pentatonic scale in any key needed.

F Minor Pentatonic Scale
(Closed Position)

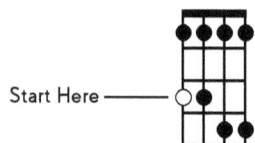

Start Here

Fingering 3 1 3 1 4 1 4 1 4 1 3 1 3 1 3

```
T
A    1  3         1    4              4  1              3  1  3
B 3            1      4      1  4  1        3  1    3
```

ALL YOUR MUSIC NEEDS

TERRYCARTERMUSICSTORE.COM

GREAT
JOB!

I want to congratulate you for getting through the Uke Like The Pros Baritone Ukulele Bootcamp book by Terry Carter. I am proud of you for making the commitment to yourself and your playing. You should have a better understanding of the Baritone Ukulele, and you can now take the next step in your playing, which is to become a Platinum Member at **ukelikethepros.com/platinum**

Platinum Members have access to over 25 Courses, Challenges, Giveaways, Workshops, and LIVE QA with the entire ULTP Community. You owe it to yourself and your playing to become a Platinum Member at **ukelikethepros.com/platinum**

THE ESSENTIALS

It is important to learn and memorize these terms and symbols because they not only apply to ukulele but to all music.

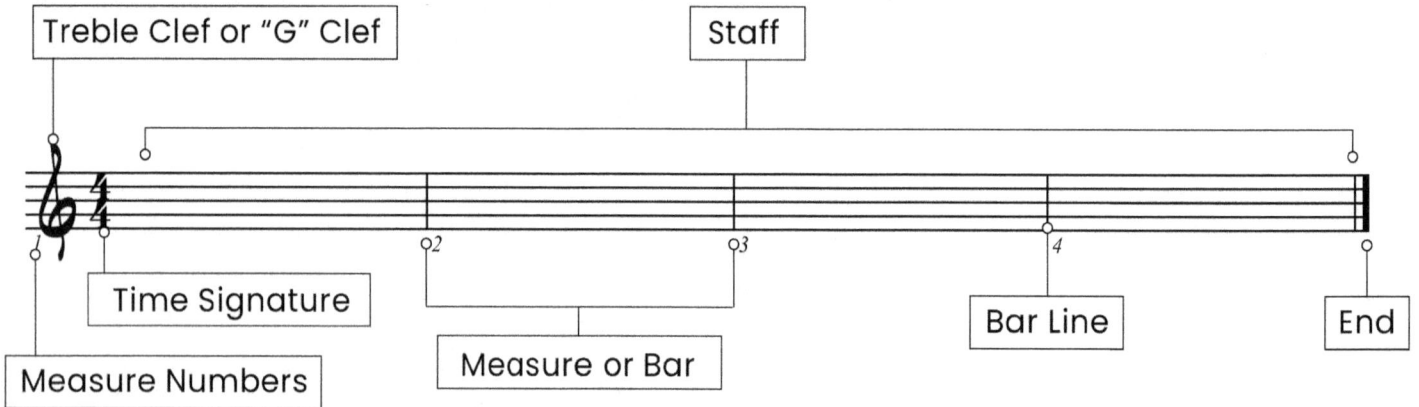

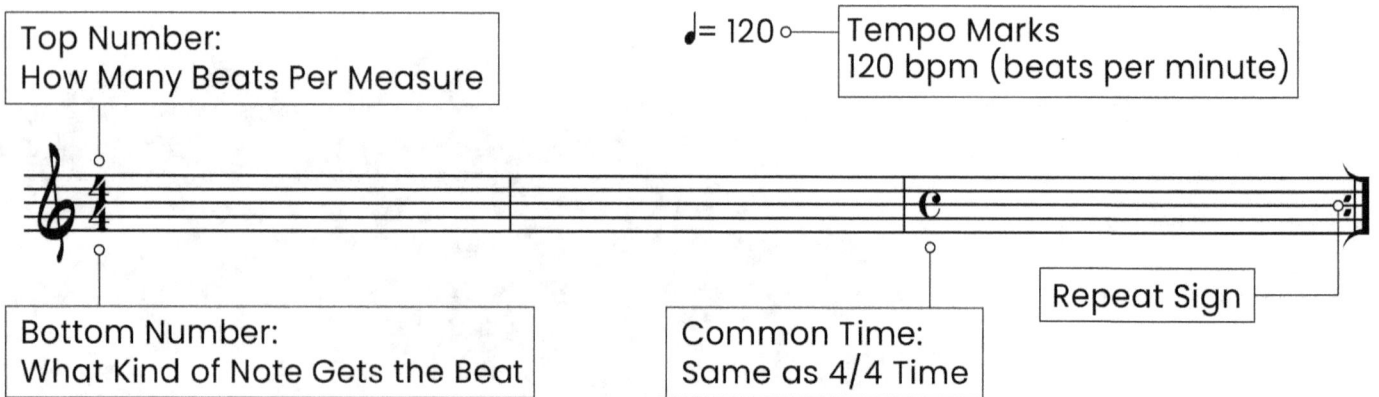

Treble Clef or "G" Clef | Staff

Time Signature

Measure Numbers

Measure or Bar

Bar Line

End

Top Number:
How Many Beats Per Measure

♩= 120 — Tempo Marks
120 bpm (beats per minute)

Bottom Number:
What Kind of Note Gets the Beat

Common Time:
Same as 4/4 Time

Repeat Sign

Notes On The Staff: There are seven notes in music (A, B, C, D, E, F, G) and they move up and down alphabetically on the staff.

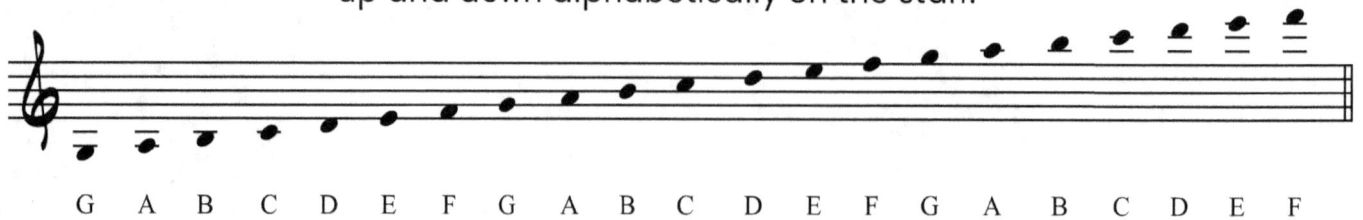

G A B C D E F G A B C D E F G A B C D E F

How To Remember The Notes:

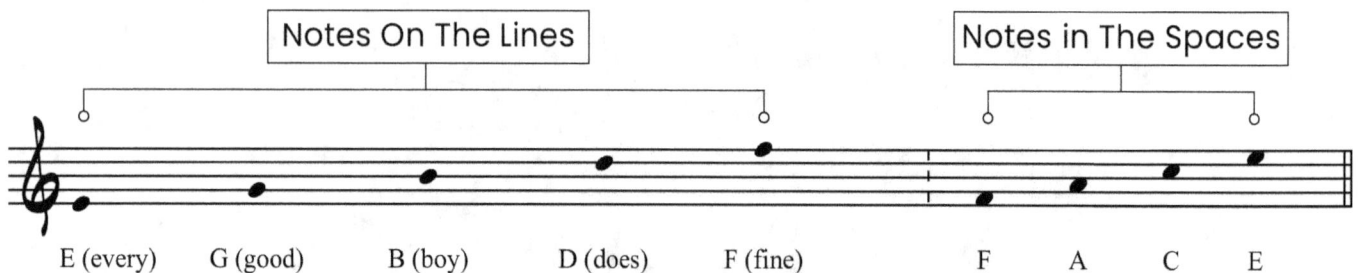

Notes On The Lines

Notes in The Spaces

E (every)   G (good)   B (boy)   D (does)   F (fine)   F   A   C   E

HOW TO READ TAB

Tablature (TAB) is a form of music reading for the baritone ukulele that uses a 4 line staff and numbers. Each line of the staff represents a string on the baritone and the numbers represent which fret you play on. When looking at the TAB staff it reads like it's upside down on the paper compared to the strings of your baritone. On the TAB staff, the highest line (closest to the sky) represents the 1st string (E string) of the baritone, while the lowest line (closest to the ground) represents the 4th string (D string) of the baritone. When you see 2 or more notes stacked on top of each other on the TAB staff, that means you play those notes at the same time, like a chord.

BARITONE STRINGS

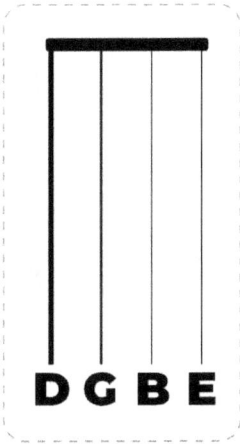

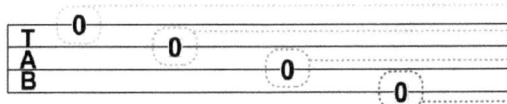

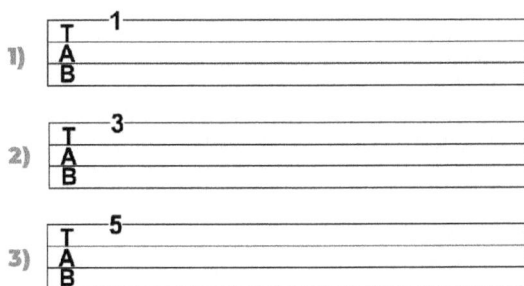

1rst STRING EXAMPLES

1) E string. FIRST FRET.
2) E string. THIRD FRET.
3) E string. FIFTH FRET.

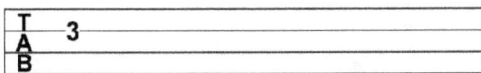

2nd STRING - B string. THIRD FRET.

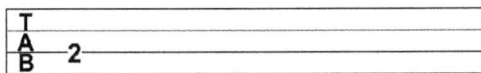

3rd STRING - G string. SECOND FRET.

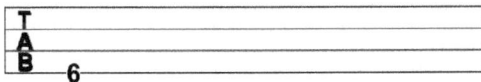

4th STRING - D string. SIXTH FRET.

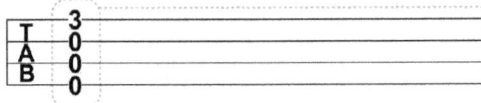

CHORD

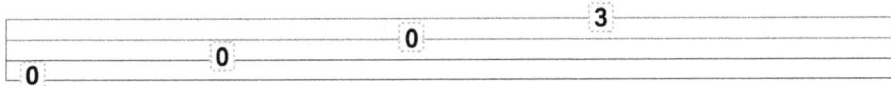

ARPEGGIO
USING THE G CHORD

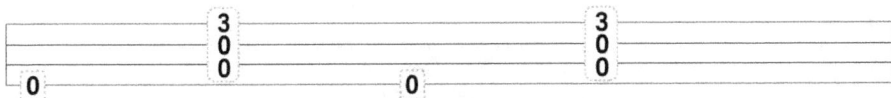

PINCH
USING THE G CHORD

B

BARITONE UKULELE PARTS

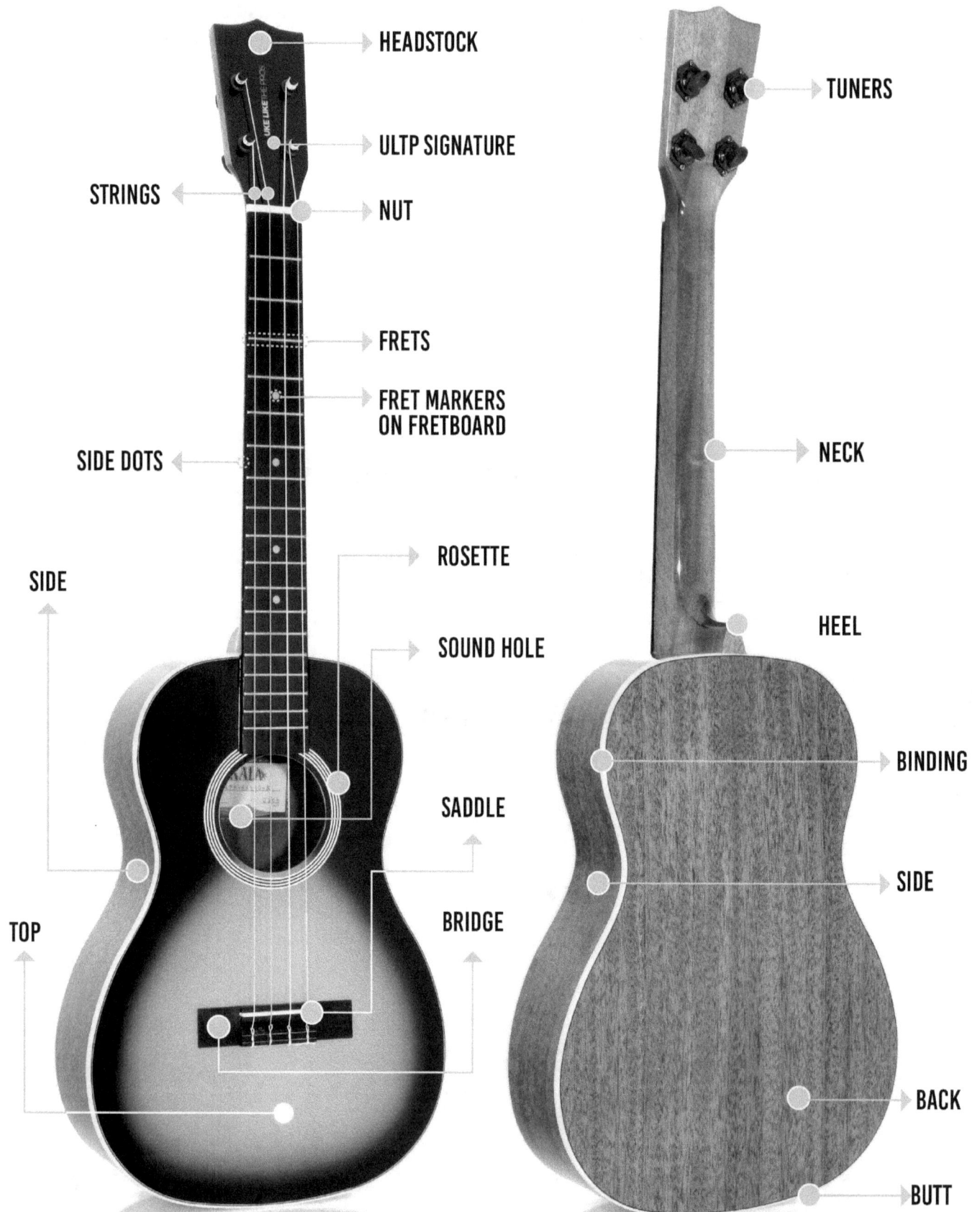

HEADSTOCK

ULTP SIGNATURE

STRINGS

NUT

FRETS

FRET MARKERS
ON FRETBOARD

SIDE DOTS

ROSETTE

SIDE

SOUND HOLE

SADDLE

TOP

BRIDGE

TUNERS

NECK

HEEL

BINDING

SIDE

BACK

BUTT

BARITONE HANDS

When playing fingerstyle on your baritone ukulele, you will see both letters and numbers to indicate which fingers to use both for your picking hand and your fretting hand. These letters and numbers will show up in the music notation, TAB, and/or chord diagrams.

FRETTING HAND	PICKING HAND
The left hand for right-handed players. will be indicated in the music or chord diagrams by numbers:	The right hand for right-handed players. will be indicated in the music by letters:
1=Index finger **3**=Ring finger	**p**=Thumb **m**=Middle
2=Middle finger **4**=Pinky finger	**i**=Index **a**= Ring **c**=pinky (not used in this course)

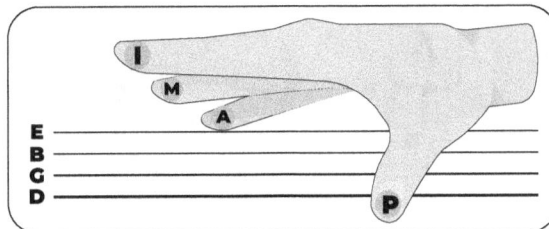

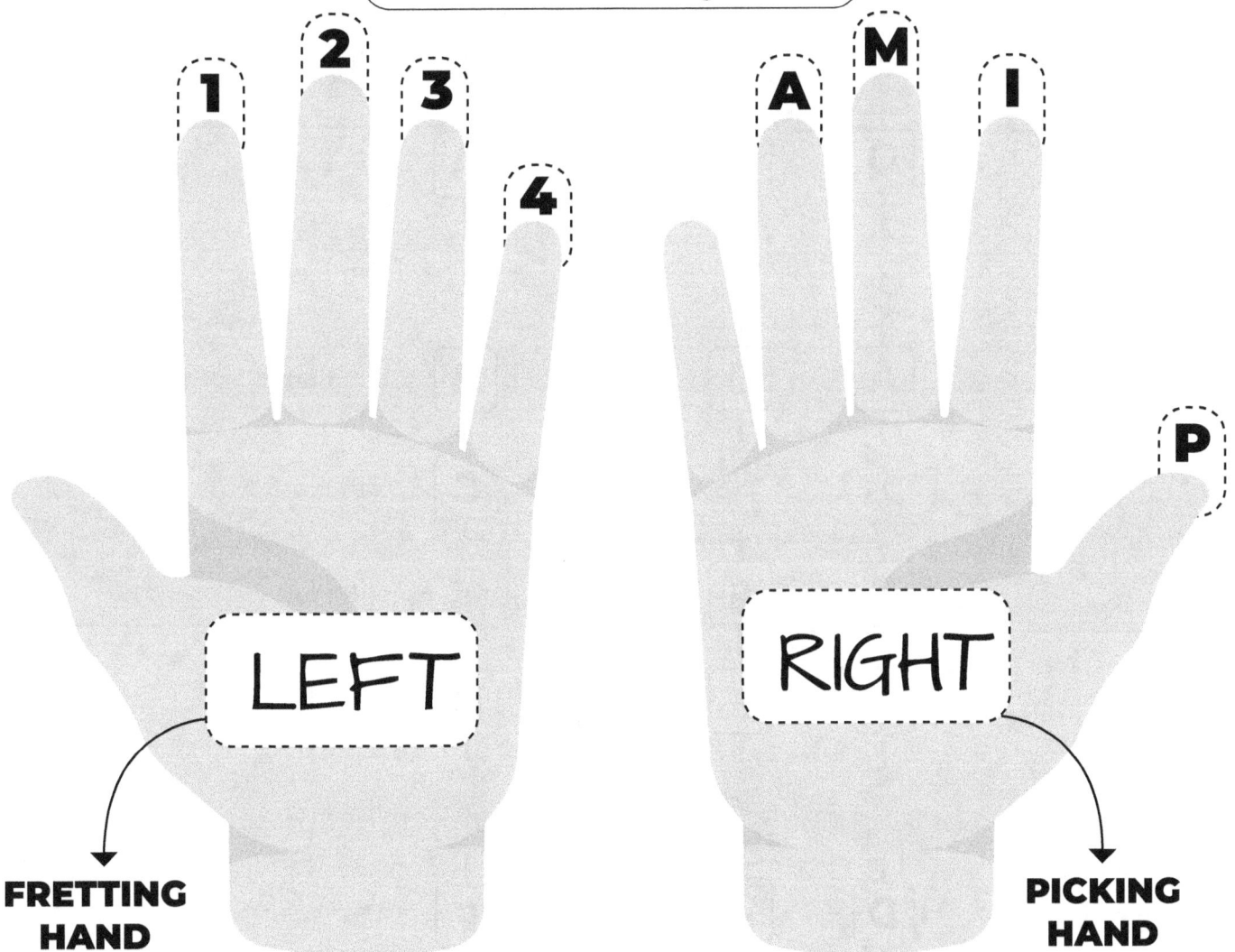

LEFT

RIGHT

FRETTING HAND

PICKING HAND

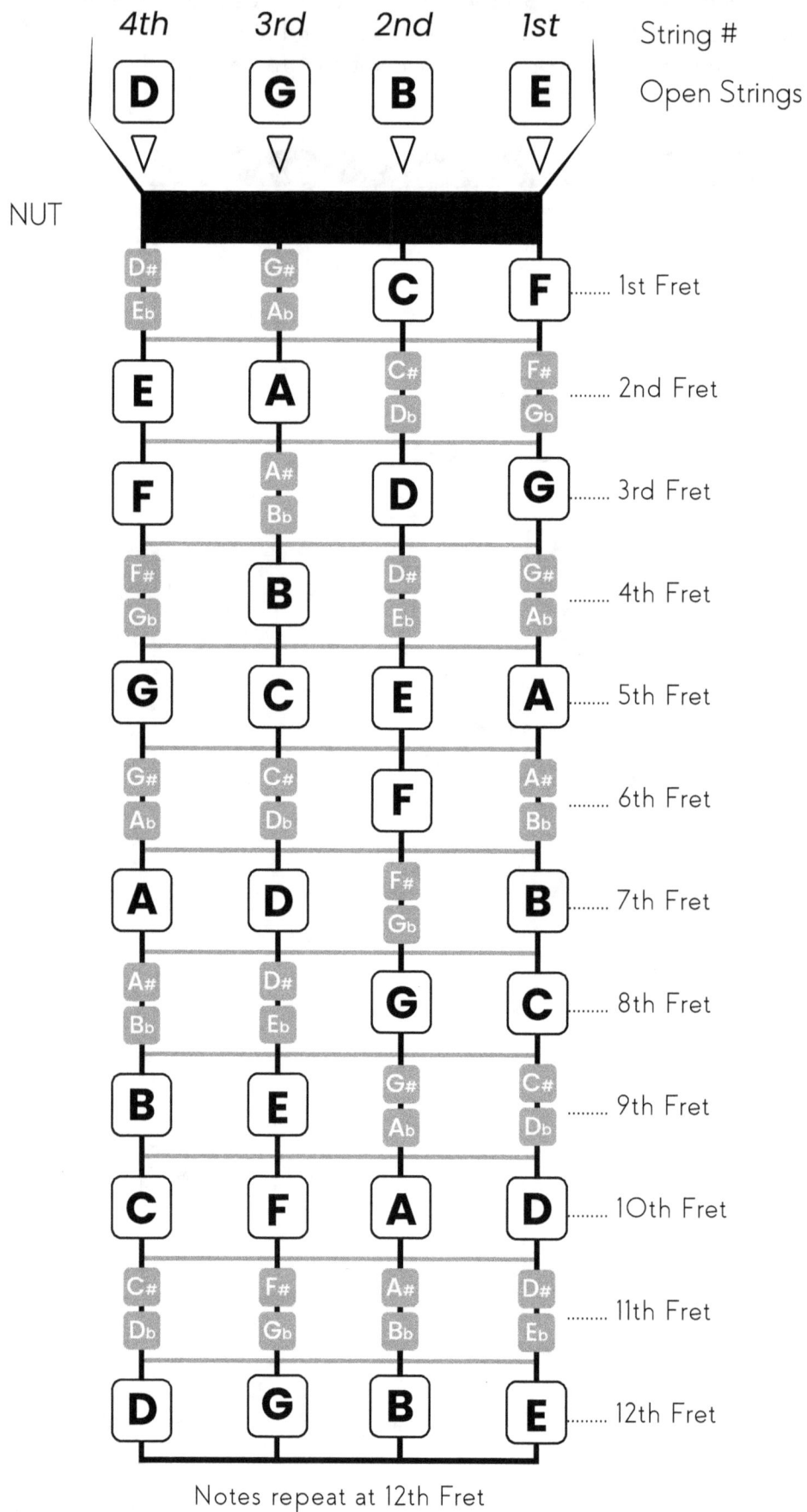

NOTES ON THE BARITONE NECK
UKULELE

	4th	3rd	2nd	1st	
String #					
Open Strings	D	G	B	E	
NUT					
1st Fret	D# / Eb	G# / Ab	C	F	
2nd Fret	E	A	C# / Db	F# / Gb	
3rd Fret	F	A# / Bb	D	G	
4th Fret	F# / Gb	B	D# / Eb	G# / Ab	
5th Fret	G	C	E	A	
6th Fret	G# / Ab	C# / Db	F	A# / Bb	
7th Fret	A	D	F# / Gb	B	
8th Fret	A# / Bb	D# / Eb	G	C	
9th Fret	B	E	G# / Ab	C# / Db	
10th Fret	C	F	A	D	
11th Fret	C# / Db	F# / Gb	A# / Bb	D# / Eb	
12th Fret	D	G	B	E	

Notes repeat at 12th Fret

UNDERSTANDING CHORD DIAGRAMS

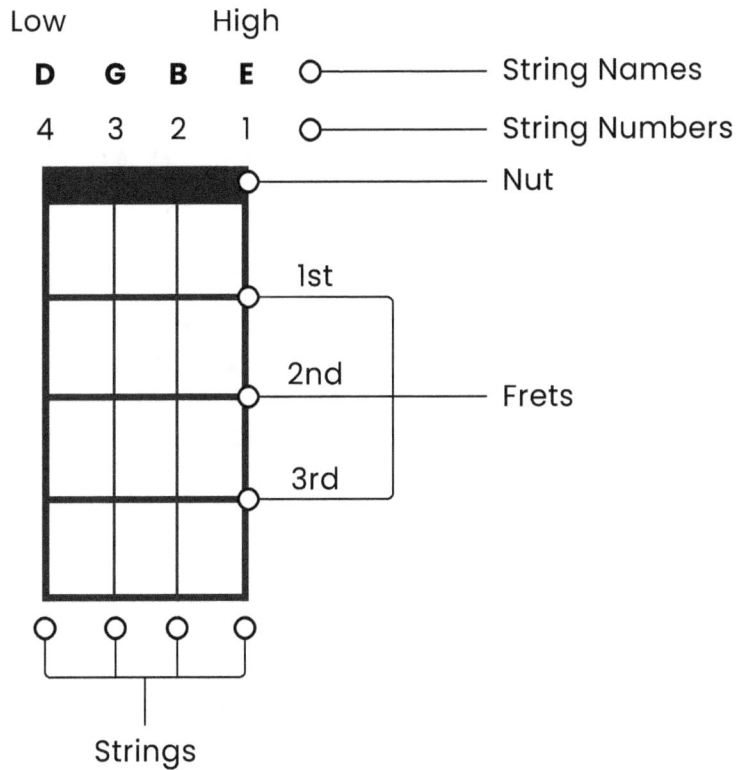

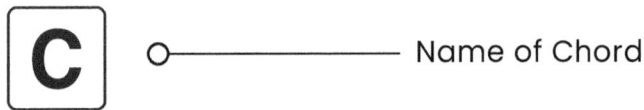

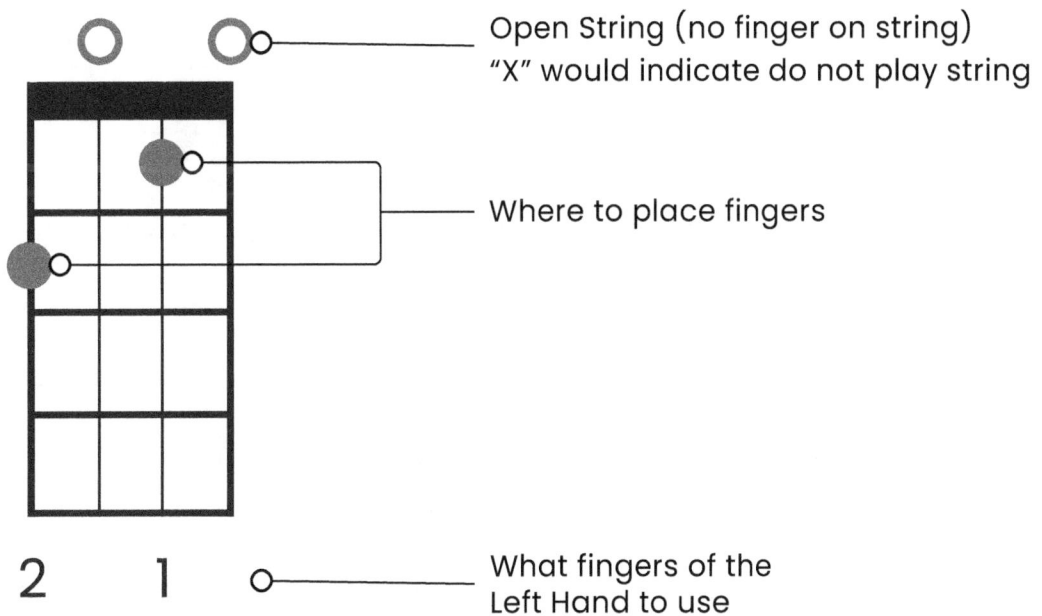

Low | High
D   G   B   E   ○ ——— String Names
4   3   2   1   ○ ——— String Numbers

——— Nut

1st

2nd   ——— Frets

3rd

Strings

C   ○ ——— Name of Chord

○   ○ ——— Open String (no finger on string)
          "X" would indicate do not play string

——— Where to place fingers

2   1   ○ ——— What fingers of the
          Left Hand to use

F

MUSIC SYMBOLS TO KNOW

A variety of symbols, articulations, repeats, hammer on's, pull off's, bends, and slides.

Fermata:
Hold note

Staccato:
Play note short

Accent:
Play note loud

Accented Staccato:
Play note
loud + short

Vibrato
Rapid "shaking"
of note

Arpeggiated Chord:
Play the notes in fast
succession from low
to high strings

Grace Note:
Fast embellishment
note played before
the main note

Mute:
"Muffle" sound of
strings either with
left or right hand

Down Stroke:
Pick string(s) with a
downward motion

Up Stroke:
Pick string(s) with
an upward motion

Tie:
Play first note but
do not play second
note that it is tied to

Ledger Lines:
Extend the staff
higher or lower.

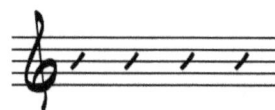

Slash Notation:
Repeat notes & rhythms
from previous measure

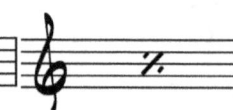

1 Bar Repeat:
Repeat notes &
rhythms from
previous measure

2 Bar Repeat:
Repeat notes & rhythms
from previous 2 measures

Repeat Sign:
(Beginning)

Repeat Sign:
(End)

1st Ending:
Play this part the
first time only

2nd Ending:
Play this part
the second time

(D.C. AL FINE) — *D.C.* (da capo) means go to the beginning of the tune and stop when you get to *Fine*

(D.C. AL CODA) — *D.C.* means go to the beginning of the tune and jump to *Coda* ⊕ when you see the sign ⊕

(D.S. AL FINE) — *D.S.* (dal segno) means go to the *Sign* 𝄋 and stop when you get to *Fine*

(D.S. AL CODA) — *D.S.* means go to the *Sign* 𝄋 And Jump to the *Coda* ⊕ when you see ⊕

SIM... — Play the same rhythm, strum pattern, or picking pattern as the previous measure

ETC... — Continue the same rhythm, strum pattern, or picking pattern as the previous measure

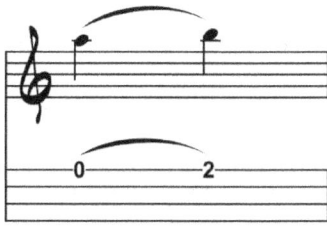

Hammer On:
Pick first note then hammer on
to the next note without picking it.

Pull Off:
Pick first note then pull off to
the next note without picking it.

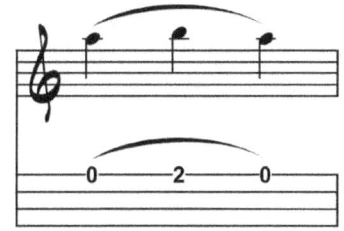

Hammer On & Pull Off:
Pick first note, hammer on to the
next note, and pull off to the last
note all in one motion.

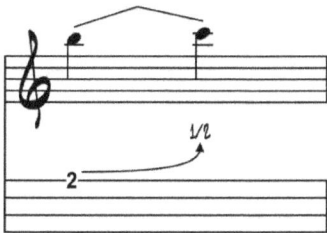

1/2 Step Bend:
Bend the first note
a 1/2 step or 1 fret.

Whole Step Bend:
Bend the first note a whole
step or 2 frets.

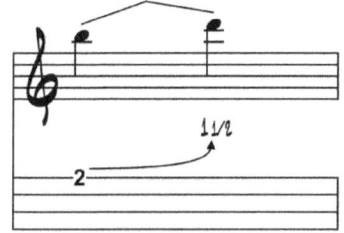

Step & 1/2 Bend:
Bend the first note
1 1/2 steps or 3 frets.

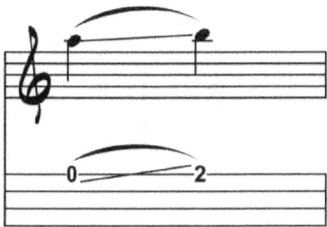

Forward Slide:
Pick first note and slide
up to higher note.

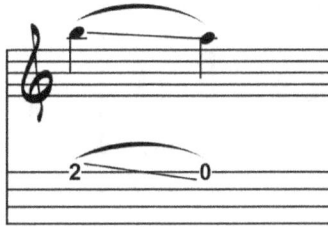

Backward Slide:
Pick first note and
slide back to lower note.

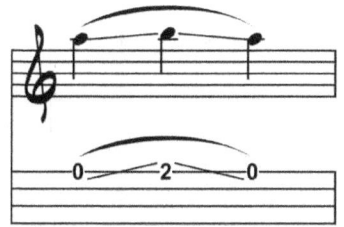

Forward/Backward Slide:
Pick first note, slide up to
next note and then slide back.

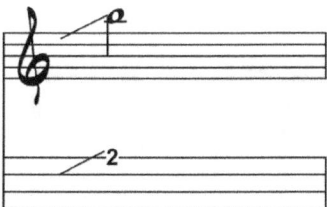

Slide Into Note:
Slide from 2-3 frets below note.

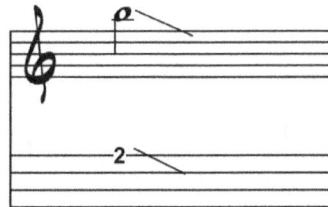

Slide Off Note:
Slide off 2-5 frets after note.

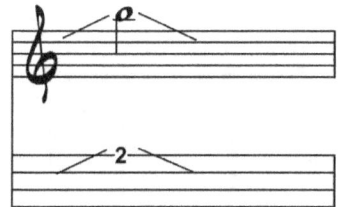

**Slide Into Note
then Slide Off Note.**

BARITONE CHORD CHART

These are some of the most widely used chords in all of music. Although there are more chords than what is listed, these chords represent the most widely used shapes.

MAJOR CHORDS

A — 1 1 2
B — 2 2 3 1
C — 2 1
D — 1 3 2
E — 2 1
F — 3 2 1 1
G — 3

MINOR CHORDS

Amin — 2 3 1
Bmin — 3 4 2 1 (2nd FRET)
Cmin — 3 4 2 1 (3rd FRET)
Dmin — 2 3 1
Emin — 2
Fmin — 3 1 1 1
Gmin — 3 1 1 1 (3rd FRET)

DOMINANT 7th CHORDS

A⁷ — 2 3
B⁷ — 1 2 3
C⁷ — 2 3 1 4
D⁷ — 2 1 3
E⁷ — 1
F⁷ — 1 2 1 1
G⁷ — 1

MAJOR 7th CHORDS

A maj7	B maj7	C maj7	D maj7	E maj7	F maj7	G maj7

C maj7 — 5th FRET

| 1 1 1 3 | 1 3 2 | 2 3 | 1 1 1 | 1 3 3 3 | 3 2 1 | 2 |

MINOR 7th CHORDS

A min7	B min7	C min7	D min7	E min7	F min7	G min7

| 2 3 1 4 | 2 3 | 1 3 1 4 | 2 1 1 | 1 4 2 3 | 1 1 1 1 | 1 1 1 1 |

SUS + ADD CHORDS

A sus4	B sus4	C add4	D sus4	E sus4	F sus4	G sus4

B sus4 — 2nd FRET

| 1 1 3 | 2 3 4 1 | 3 1 | 1 3 4 | 2 3 | 3 4 1 1 | 1 3 |

BEGINNING STRUM PATTERNS

These 4 rhythms, the whole note (rings for 4 beats), the half note (rings for 2 beats), the quarter note (rings for 1 beat), and the eighth note (rings for ½ a beat) make up the most important strum patterns for ukulele. Study and memorize these rhythms and strum patterns.

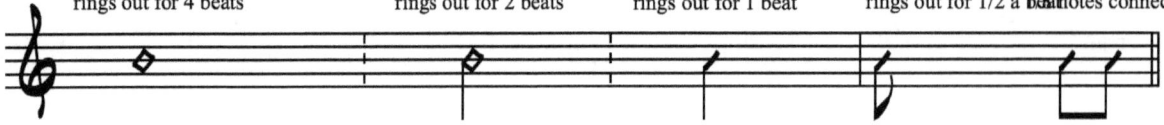

ABOUT THE AUTHOR

Terry Carter is a San Diego-based ukulele player, surfer, songwriter, and creator of ukelikethepros.com, rock-likethepros.com and terrycartermusicstore.com. With over 25 years as a professional musician, educator and Los Angeles studio musician, Terry has worked with greats like Weezer, Josh Groban, Robby Krieger (The Doors), 2-time Grammy winning composer Christopher Tin (Calling All Dawns), Duff McKagan (Guns N' Roses), Grammy winning producer Charles Goodan (Santana/ Rolling Stones), and the Los Angeles Philharmonic. Terry has written and produced tracks for commercials (Discount Tire and Puma) and TV shows, including Scorpion (CBS), Pit Bulls & Parolees (Animal Planet), Trippin', Wildboyz, and The Real World (MTV). He has self-published over 25 books for Uke Like The Pros and Rock Like The Pros, filmed over 30 ukulele and guitar online courses, and has tens of millions of views on his docial media channels.

Terry received a Master of Music in Studio/Jazz Guitar Performance from University of Southern California and a Bachelor of Music from San Diego State University, with an emphasis in Jazz Studies and Music Education. He has taught at the University of Southern California, San Diego State University, Santa Monica College, Miracosta College, and Los Angeles Trade Tech College.

TERRY CARTER MUSIC STORE

All your music needs at the #1 music store, **terrycartermusicstore.com**

Baritones

Ukuleles

Guitars

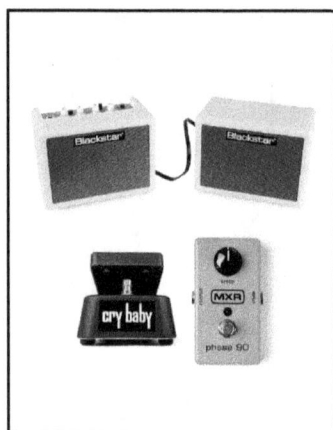

Amplifiers and
Pedals

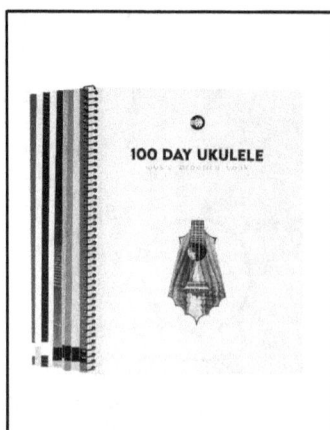

Books

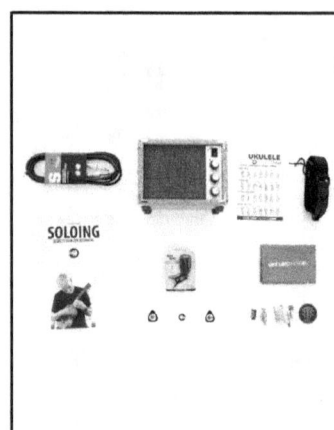

Accessories

ONLINE UKULELE COURSES

The perfect place to learn how to play Ukulele, Baritone Ukulele, Guitar and Guitarlele.

ULTP Roadmap
WHERE TO START?

1) UKULELE BEGINNER
A.   Beginning Ukulele Starter Course
B.   Beginning Ukulele Bootcamp Course
C.   Ukulele Fundamentals Course
D.   Ukulele Practice & Technique Course
E.   Master the Ukulele 1

2) UKULELE INTERMEDIATE
A.   Master The Ukulele 2
B.   Beginning Music Reading
C.   23 Ultimate Chord Progressions
D.   Beginning Ukulele Fingerstyle Course

3) UKULELE ADVANCED
A.   Ukulele Blues Mastery Course
B.   Beginning Ukulele Soloing Course
C.   Fingerstyle Mastery Course
D.   Jazz Swing Mastery Course

MORE OPTIONS!

FUNLAND
A.   Beginning Ukulele Kids Course Songbook
B.   21 Popular Songs for Ukulele
C.   The Best Ukulele Christmas Songs
D.   10 Classic Rock Licks
E.   Guitar Fundamentals

BARITONE UKULELE
A.   Beginning Baritone Ukulele Bootcamp Course
B.   6 Weeks Baritone Q&A
C.   Baritone Blues Mastery Course
D.   Beginning Baritone Fingerstyle Course

GUITARLELE
A.   Guitarlele Starter Course
B.   6 Weeks Guitarlele Q&A
C.   Guitarlele Course for Ukulele and Guitar Players
D.   Guitarlele Blues Mastery Course

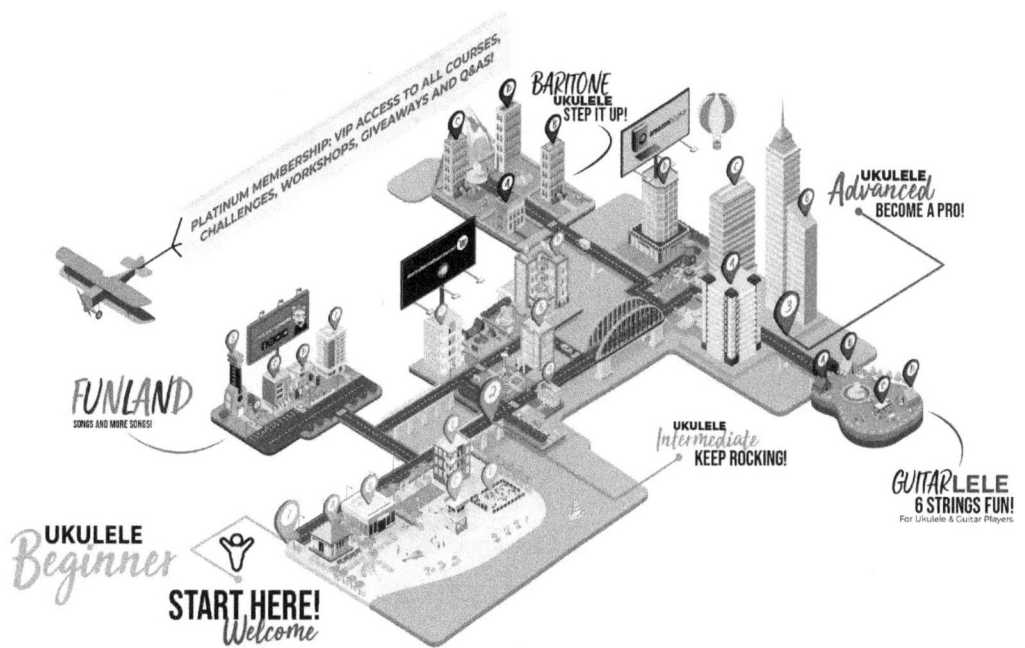

PLATINUM MEMBERSHIP: VIP ACCESS TO ALL COURSES, CHALLENGES, WORKSHOPS, GIVEAWAYS AND Q&AS!

BARITONE UKULELE STEP IT UP!

UKULELE *Advanced* BECOME A PRO!

FUNLAND SONGS AND MORE SONGS!

UKULELE *Intermediate* KEEP ROCKING!

GUITARLELE 6 STRINGS FUN! For Ukulele & Guitar Players

UKULELE *Beginner*

START HERE! Welcome

GUITARLELE BLUES MASTERY COURSE

UKULELE MUSIC READING COURSE

23 ULTIMATE CHORD PROGRESSIONS COURSE

GUITARLELE FOR UKULELE & GUITAR PLAYERS COURSE

BEGINNING UKULELE SOLOING COURSE

CHRISTMAS SONGS FOR UKULELE COURSE

BEGINNING UKULELE BOOTCAMP COURSE

BEGINNING BARITONE UKULELE BOOTCAMP

BEGINNING UKULELE STARTER COURSE

21 POPULAR SONGS FOR UKULELE

BEGINNING BARITONE FINGERSTYLE COURSE

INTERMEDIATE MASTER THE UKULELE #2 COURSE

BEGINNING PRACTICE & TECHNIQUE BOOTCAMP

UKULELE FINGERSTYLE COURSE

BEGINNING UKULELE FINGERSTYLE COURSE

UKULELE BLUES MASTERY COURSE

BARITONE BLUES MASTERY COURSE

BEGINNING MASTER THE UKULELE #1 COURSE

JAZZ SWING MASTERY #1 COURSE

KIDS UKULELE COURSE

Courses For All Levels
UKELIKETHEPROS.COM

N

UKELIKETHEPROS.COM
BLOG.UKELIKETHEPROS.COM
TERRYCARTERMUSICSTORE.COM
BUYSTRINGSONLINE.COM

@ukelikethepros

INTERESTED IN **GUITAR CONTENT?**
ROCKLIKETHEPROS.COM

www.ingramcontent.com/pod-product-compliance
Lightning Source LLC
LaVergne TN
LVHW081322060426
835509LV00015B/1645